You Let the Cat Out of the Bag!

(And Other Crazy Animal Sayings)

written by Cynthia Klingel ★ illustrated by Mernie Gallagher-Cole

ABOUT THE AUTHOR

As a high school English teacher and as an elementary teacher, Cynthia Klingel has shared her love of language with students. She has always been fascinated with idioms and figures of speech. Today Cynthia is a school district administrator in Minnesota. She has two daughters who also share her love of language through reading, writing, and talking!

ABOUT THE ILLUSTRATOR

Mernie Gallagher-Cole lives in Pennsylvania with her husband and two children. She uses sayings and phrases like the ones in this book every day. She has illustrated many children's books, including *Messy Molly* and *Día De Los Muertos* for The Child's World®.

The Child's World®

Published in the United States of America by The Child's World®
1980 Lookout Drive • Mankato, MN 56003-1705
800-599-READ • www.childsworld.com

ACKNOWLEDGMENTS
The Child's World®: Mary Berendes, Publishing Director

The Creative Spark: Editing

The Design Lab: Kathleen Petelinsek, Design and Page Production

LIBRARY OF CONGRESS CATALOGING-IN-PUBLICATION DATA
Klingel, Cynthia Fitterer.
You let the cat out of the bag!: (and other crazy animal sayings) / by Cynthia Klingel.
    p. cm.—(Sayings and phrases)
  ISBN-13: 978-1-59296-903-6 (lib. bdg.: alk. paper)
  ISBN-10: 1-59296-903-8 (lib. bdg.: alk. paper)
1. English language—Idioms—Juvenile literature.
2. Figures of speech—Juvenile literature. I. Title.
II. Series.
PE1460.K685 2007
428—dc22   2007004215

People use idioms *(ID-ee-umz) every day. These are sayings and phrases with meanings that are different from the actual words. Some idioms seem silly. Many of them don't make much sense . . . at first.*

This book will help you understand some of the most common idioms. It will tell you how you might hear a saying or phrase. It will tell you what the saying really means. All of these sayings and short phrases—even the silly ones—are an important part of our language!

TABLE *of* CONTENTS

Bats in the belfry

Rita and Charlie were reading another e-mail from Aunt Martha. This time she was traveling to Mexico. Her e-mails were always filled with crazy stories about her trips. Rita and Charlie never knew whether to believe her or not.

"That Aunt Martha," said Rita. "Sometimes I think she has bats in her belfry."

MEANING: To have crazy ideas; to be confused

Birds of a feather flock together

Katie was having a party. She invited people who were fun and liked being together. They were having a great time. They ate and ate. They watched movies. Then they talked.

"Hey!" exclaimed Carly. "Everybody here plays volleyball. I just realized that."

"You're right," agreed Katie. "I guess birds of a feather flock together."

MEANING: People who like the same things or who think alike often become friends and do things together.

Bring home the bacon

Ryan wanted a cell phone. He also wanted a new computer.

"How much money have you saved?" asked Mom.

"Not enough," answered Ryan.

"Those are expensive things, Ryan," said Mom. "I can't afford to spend that much right now. If you want those things, you're going to have to get a job. You need to start bringing home the bacon, too."

MEANING: To earn money. An older meaning is to win a game or prize.

5

Can't hold a candle to

Sally's family loved playing horseshoes. Sally liked it because she was really good! Today's game was fierce. Her brother, Tad, was determined to win. But the game was not going his way.

"Nice game, Tad!" congratulated his dad. "You came so close. But it looks like Sally beat everyone again. Tad, you can beat us all when it comes to playing cards, but in horseshoes, we can't hold a candle to Sally!"

MEANING: Not as good as something or someone else; not having the same skill as someone else

Cry over spilled milk

Kris grabbed the stack of papers and shredded them. That was her job, and she was in a hurry to get outside.

Harry looked at the table. His paper for English was gone.

"Hey! Where's my paper?" asked Harry.

"If it was on the table with the stack of recycling, it's in the shredder now," answered Kris.

Harry was mad. How could she do that? He'd worked so hard!

"Oh, Harry. Stop crying over spilled milk. You did it on the computer. Just print another copy."

MEANING: To complain about something that is over and done with; to be upset about something that can't be changed

Dog days of summer

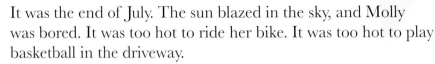

It was the end of July. The sun blazed in the sky, and Molly was bored. It was too hot to ride her bike. It was too hot to play basketball in the driveway.

"These are the dog days of summer," said Molly's mom. "Remember them when you are having a busy day at school in the fall!"

MEANING: The time during summer that is very hot, when the days seem long

A drop in the bucket

Steven had been saving up for new in-line skates. He wanted the best pair he could get. But he had to admit that he hadn't been very good at saving.

"Mom, I've saved five dollars so far. How much more will I need?" asked Steven.

"Five dollars?" asked Mom. "It's going to be a while before you have enough. That's just a drop in the bucket!"

MEANING: Not very much; only a start on something that needs a lot more

8

Egg on your face

Carrie had been bragging about the huge birthday party she was going to have. She told all her classmates they were being invited to a concert. Before the concert would be a pizza party. They would go to the concert in a fancy car, too! The problem was, Carrie hadn't bothered to ask her parents about having such a party. Guess what they said? Absolutely not! Carrie had to go to school and tell everyone that there wouldn't be such a fancy party. Carrie was very embarrassed.

"I'm sorry to hear that, Carrie," said Mom. "It's not easy when you have egg on your face. Hopefully you've learned a lesson from all of this."

MEANING: To be embarrassed; to look foolish in front of others, especially if it's from being wrong

Fish or cut bait

Tryouts for the city youth band were tomorrow. Brady needed to learn to play three different songs on his clarinet. So far he'd only practiced one. He just wasn't sure he wanted to be in the band. One minute he wanted to and he'd start practicing. The next minute he didn't want to and he'd do something else. He just couldn't decide.

"I don't know what you're thinking, Brady," sighed his mom. "You need to either fish or cut bait."

MEANING: To make a decision, especially if it has taken you a long time to make up your mind

Fly off the handle

Dad walked in the door from work. He looked tired.

"Boy, am I glad to be home!" exclaimed Dad. "Things are so stressful at work. I just can't believe how people are acting. If one more person flies off the handle, I don't know what I'm going to do!"

MEANING: To become upset or throw a tantrum; to act out of control, especially if you're angry

Get your goat

Ben was running out of patience. His little sister was bothering him on purpose. He couldn't take one more minute.

"Mom!" called Ben. "I'm trying to do my homework and Ella won't leave me alone. She's doing everything she can think of to annoy me. Will you please make her stop?"

"Don't let her get your goat, Ben," said Mom. "Just ignore her and she'll get bored and go away."

MEANING: To bother or annoy

Go the extra mile

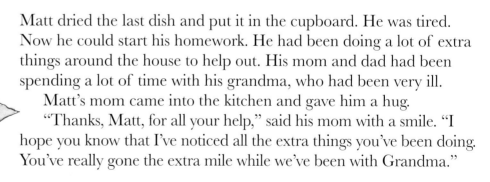

Matt dried the last dish and put it in the cupboard. He was tired. Now he could start his homework. He had been doing a lot of extra things around the house to help out. His mom and dad had been spending a lot of time with his grandma, who had been very ill.

Matt's mom came into the kitchen and gave him a hug.

"Thanks, Matt, for all your help," said his mom with a smile. "I hope you know that I've noticed all the extra things you've been doing. You've really gone the extra mile while we've been with Grandma."

MEANING: To do more than is expected of you; to do more than you have to

Hit the nail on the head

Jacob was frustrated with the puzzle. He and Hattie had been working on it for hours. He just couldn't finish the part he was working on. He knew the piece he needed was there, but he just couldn't find it!

"Let me look," said Hattie. "I think it will have some red in the middle. See the picture?"

"You're right!" exclaimed Jacob. "You've hit the nail on the head. Here's the piece, right in front of me!"

MEANING: To be exactly right; to figure something out

In one ear and out the other

Mom carefully opened the door of Maggie's bedroom. Maggie had agreed that she would clean her messy room before she went to her friend's birthday party. But Maggie's mom gasped at the sight—the room was still a disaster!

Just then Dad walked up behind her. "What's wrong?" he asked.

"I told Maggie she needed to clean this mess before going to the party!" Mom explained. "You know, it seems that anything I tell her just goes in one ear and out the other!"

MEANING: To ignore or forget something that you've been told; not to do something you've been told to do

13

Keep your nose to the grindstone

Carlo wanted to be on the honor roll. But he'd been too busy hanging out with friends. He hadn't been spending as much time on his homework as he needed.

"You still have a chance," his older brother encouraged him. "You just need to keep your nose to the grindstone."

MEANING: To work hard

Left out in the cold

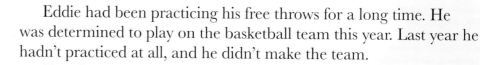

Eddie had been practicing his free throws for a long time. He was determined to play on the basketball team this year. Last year he hadn't practiced at all, and he didn't make the team.

"Aren't you getting sick of standing there and throwing that ball over and over?" asked his friend Terry.

"No way!" answered Eddie. "I'm making sure my free throws are solid. This year I'm going to make the team. Last year I was left out in the cold. That isn't going to happen again this year!"

MEANING: Not to be included in something; to be left out

Let the cat out of the bag

Jack's mom and dad were excited. They had planned a surprise party for Jack's birthday. One night the phone rang and Jack answered. As he listened to his friend, Dana, his eyes grew huge! A grin appeared and stretched from ear to ear. He quickly hung up the phone, jumping and shouting, "YES! A birthday party! I'm having a birthday party! Thank you, Mom and Dad!"

Mom and Dad were speechless. They couldn't believe it! Dana had let the cat out of the bag. The party would no longer be a surprise!

MEANING: To tell a secret

Long in the tooth

Today was Grandpa's birthday. Everyone had arrived at Frank's house for the party. It had been a great party, so far. Now was time for the cake.

"Hey, Grandpa," asked Frank. "How old are you?"

"I'm eighty-five," answered Grandpa.

"That's old!" exclaimed Frank.

"I'm getting long in the tooth," said Grandpa with a chuckle. "I bet you can't even imagine what it's like to be eighty-five years old!"

MEANING: To be old

Nip it in the bud

Harry was grounded. He knew he would be in trouble the minute he walked in the door.

"Do you think we should have given him another chance?" Harry's mom asked his dad.

"No, I don't," answered his dad. "Harry should know better. I think that grounding was the right thing to do. We need to nip this in the bud."

MEANING: To stop something or correct something right away before it gets worse

Once in a blue moon

Nate and Mandy were bored. They needed something exciting to do.

"Hey! I've got an idea," exclaimed Nate. "We could ride our bikes to the mall. Does your mom ever let you ride that far?"

"Are you kidding? Only once in a blue moon. We can ask her, though. Maybe this is one of the times she'll let me," answered Mandy.

MEANING: When something doesn't happen very often; when there's not a very good chance that something will happen

Pay through the nose

A new game had just come out for Olivia's electronic game station. She couldn't wait to get it. She begged her brother to drive her to the store.

"Just be patient," replied her brother. "If you buy it now, you're going to pay through the nose. Just wait a little while until it goes on sale."

MEANING: To pay a lot for something; to pay more for something than you should

Pull a fast one

Mom couldn't believe the surprise for her birthday. She had no idea her family was planning a trip to the beach for the weekend! She had just opened a card with the plane ticket inside.

"You are all very clever," she said with a smile. "I had no idea! You really pulled a fast one on me. But I'm very glad you did!"

MEANING: To be tricky or clever; to do something that no one expected

Rain check

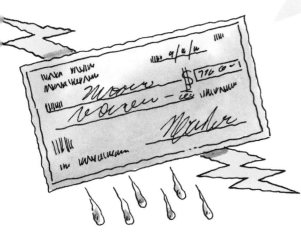

Dad looked tired. Penny thought about what she could do for him. She had an idea.

"Hey, Dad," said Penny. "I know you like neck rubs. Do you want me to give you one right now?"

"Oh, that sounds good," said Dad with a smile. "But I need to run and pick up your brother. How about if I take a rain check for now? You can give me one when I get home."

MEANING: Not to accept something at the moment, but to get it later; to wait to do something at another time

Roll with the punches

Joey and his parents sat in his classroom. It was his conference with the teacher. They had just moved to this new school a few weeks ago.

"I'm so proud of how well Joey is doing," said Ms. Alvarez, Joey's teacher. "It's not easy starting a new school in the middle of the year. But Joey just rolls with the punches."

MEANING: Not to let things bother you or get you down; to deal with things that happen and just move on

19

A shot in the arm

"Sam!" called Tanya as she ran into the backyard. "Guess who called?"

"I give up," answered Sam. "Who?"

"Do you remember that writing contest I entered? Well, they just called to tell me I made the top three! I get to go to a big dinner for the winners! We'll find out there who got first prize!" exclaimed Tanya.

"Congratulations! That's a real shot in the arm. I'm proud of you," said Sam with a smile.

MEANING: Something that gives you encouragement, makes you hopeful, or gives you confidence

Skeletons in the closet

Peyton's mom was running for mayor. He was helping his dad put up signs. Right now, his dad was visiting with the neighbor.

"Sure, you can put a sign for Jean in my yard," agreed the neighbor. "She's got my vote. I know she has no skeletons in the closet!"

MEANING: Something from your past that you don't want known

Step on it

It was not a good morning. Everyone was running late. Andy and Rob had already missed the bus. Dad was giving them a ride to school, but that would make him even later for work.

"Come on, guys," begged Dad. "It's getting even later. Let's step on it!"

MEANING: To hurry up

Take the bull by the horns

Erin had been very excited when the team voted her one of the volleyball co-captains. But it had not been fun so far. The other co-captain, Shelly, had been so bossy. The rest of the team was fed up. Now they were getting upset with Erin for not telling Shelly how they felt.

"It sounds to me," said Erin's mom, "that you need to take the bull by the horns. Your teammates voted for you. They believe in you and need you to talk to Shelly about what's happening."

MEANING: To take control of a situation; to have courage to do what needs to be done

Toe the line

It had not been a good day for Haley. In fact, it hadn't been a good week. She had gotten in trouble for something every day. Now Haley was in the office discussing her behavior with Ms. Goldberg.

"This is it, Haley," said Ms. Goldberg sternly. "I don't want one more situation like we had today. From now on you are really going to have to toe the line."

MEANING: To follow the rules; to make sure not to do anything wrong or inappropriate

Upset the apple cart

"This isn't fair!" exclaimed Tara. "I've wanted this sleepover for weeks. Why did you tell Uncle Mike and Aunt Bea that they could come for the weekend?"

"I know this upsets the apple cart. It changes what I had planned for this weekend, too. But we can have your sleepover next weekend," replied Tara's dad. "We hardly ever see Uncle Mike and his family."

MEANING: To change plans; to ruin plans that have already been made

White elephant

It was the ugliest thing Anna had ever seen. It was the color of mashed peas. It had big, goofy eyes. It had a long red tongue curling out of its lips. Worst of all, it was her birthday present from Aunt Lisa.

"What was she thinking?" asked Mom as she held the plastic frog in front of her.

"Who knows," answered Dad. "But it will make a great white elephant gift if you ever need one!"

MEANING: An object that is worth nothing or is useless, often something you get or give as a gift

24